ALCATRAZ

Federal Prison of a Lifetime

written by: J.D. Valens

TABLE OF CONTENTS

CHAPTER ONE

The History of Alcatraz

Alcatraz was a prison where criminals went to and never came out alive. Alcatraz sits on a island in the San Francisco Harbour. At Alcatraz, there has been so much history with the building and how much history that has been brought in by the criminals and what those criminals did. Some people wouldn't even know why these criminals are in this prison or what they did to deserve the ultimate torture. For the lives that these criminals took, they have to suffer the ultimate life sentence, Alcatraz.

During the years of Alcatraz, there were six main criminals that made up Alcatraz, along with several other men who were sentenced to serve out their sentences at Alcatraz. As long as these criminals were at Alcatraz, it became a proven fact that these men deserved to be here at Alcatraz, once they were there, they were to stay. Then once they have passed on from their deaths, their voices linger in the halls of the prison many years later after Alcatraz has been closed down as a penitentiary for life sentenced criminals.

There are so many men that were sentenced to Alcatraz, but there were many men who actually killed each other just to survive. For most of the criminals or inmates, its the survival of the fittest to survive this place of torture. The torture that the inmates received while at Alcatraz, it is relative to the torture they gave to their victims. The torture that the victims had died from is very relative to what the criminals or inmates received from the prison and their guards.

Alcatraz closed their doors in 1963, and then it became a museum for the public to view and experience just like all the inmates did several years before. There were hundreds of men at Alcatraz. Several tried to escape. More than half a dozen men were killed while they were trying to escape from Alcatraz. The ones that did make it out of the prison alive, well, let's say this, they didn't make it the mainland alive. They were eaten alive by sharks and other water animals in the harbour of the San Francisco Bay.

All the men that were at Alcatraz were sent there because the prisons' warren couldn't handle these men. Therefore, they sent these men to Alcatraz for their prison terms. There were many men that died at Alcatraz and their ghost still lingers in the corridors of the prison. So people may say "I don't believe in ghosts." But once you have experienced something like Alcatraz, you will think differently. The ghosts of the prison inmates linger all around the prison and will scare some people, especially if you're not a person who would've been found in a haunted house at Halloween.

Alcatraz opened in 1933 and closed in 1963. There were several men killed inside and outside of the prison. In one corridor of the prison, three men were killed when they got cornered by guards. Several other inmates hung themselves due to the insanity of being stuck in a prison cell for most of the day. The inmates got very little time in the yard, because of why they were sent to Alcatraz in the first place. There were very few inmates that had got released from Alcatraz, others were killed for trying to escape, there were a few that hung themselves, some were eaten alive by the sharks in the Harbour and others died from old age and being kept in a prison for a lifetime.

The Native American people stayed away from the island, because they believed it was cursed. They called Alcatraz Island, "Evil Island." The first person to document anything about Alcatraz or the island was Juan Manuel de Ayala in 1775, who also named one of three islands in the San Francisco Bay. He named one of those islands, "La Isla de los Alcatraces." This means in translation, "The Island of the Pelicans." French Captain Auguste Bernard Duhaut-Cilly wrote in one of his journals, "running past Alcatraces (Pelicans) Island...covered with a countless number of these birds. A gun fired over the feathered legions caused them to fly up in a great cloud and with a noise like a hurricane."

Alcatraz used to be a place where Civil War prisoners were kept in 1861. In the next years, the cannon amount increased from 85 to 105 in 1866. In the next year, 1867, another building was added to the Island. This building was a brick jailhouse. From 1868 - 1870s, Alcatraz Island was a designated long-term detention facility for military prisoners. Also among the incarcerated men at Alcatraz, there were confederates caught on the west coast, and some Hopi Native American men.

During the Spanish-American War, the population of the prison had increased from 26 inmates to well over 405 inmantes. This happened between 1905 - 1907, which was commanded by George W. McIver. After an earthquake in 1906, the civilian prisoners were transferred to Alcatraz for safe confinement. On 21 March, 1907, was designated as the Western U.S. Military prison, but then became the disciplinary barracks in 1915. The main cell block was designed and built in 1909 and completed in 1912.

On 12 October 1933, the Department of Justice obtained the island and turned the island into a Federal Bureau of Prison in August of 1934. On 11 August 1934, 134 federal prisoners were sent to Alcatraz from Leavenworth, Kansas and Santa Venetia, California. During the transportation of these men, they were heavily guarded by FBI agents, U.S. Marshalls, and several railway security officials. Most of the prisoners that were at Alacatraz were notorious bank robbers and murderers.

Some of the notorious criminals in history were Al Capone, Robert Franklin Stroudman (birdman of Alcatraz), George "Machine Gun" Kelly, Bumpy Johnson, Rafael Cancel Miranda (a member of the Puerto Rican Nationalist Party who attacked the United States Capitol building in 1954), Mickey Cohen, Arthur R. "Doc" Barker, James "Whitey" Bulger, and Alvin "Creepy" Karpis (who served more time at Alcatraz than any other inmate). The guards and their families were housed on the island as well.

There were several escape attempts by the inmates. There was a total of 36 prisoners that made 14 escape attempts, two mwn died trying twice; 23 were caught, six were shot and killed during their escape, two drowned, and five were listed as "missing and presumed drowned". On 2 May 1946, the most violent of attempts by six prisoners that led to the Battle of Alcatraz. On 11 June 1962, Frank Morris, John Anglin, and Clarence Anglin carried out one of the most intricate escapes ever devised.

The Native American people occupied Alcatraz Island on 20 November 1969, they called themselves United Indians of All Tribes, which were mostly college students from San Francisco. The occupiers (the Indians), stayed on the island for nearly two years. The indians demanded that the island's facilities have new and updated structures for an Indian educational center, ecology center and cultural center. There was a treaty that was created by the Sioux Indians and the U.S., this treaty was named the Treaty of Fort Laramie (1868). Indians of the All Tribes then claimed Alcatraz Island by the "Right of Discovery". The "Right of Discovery" drew Native Americans from everywhere across the United States, this includes the American Indian Movement urban activists from Minneapolis, Minnesota.

During the nineteen months and nine days of occupation by the Native American Indian people, several buildings at Alcatraz were damaged or destroyed by fire, icluding the recreation hall, the Coast Guard quarters and the warden's home. The U.S. government demolished a number of buildings, mostly apartments after the occupation of the Native Americans had ended. At many locations on the island, you can still see some of the graffiti that was done by the Native Americans. During President Richard Nixon's presidency, he rescinded the Indian termination policy, that was designed by earlier administration to end federal recognition of tribes and their special relationship with the US government.

CHAPTER TWO

Robert "Birdman" Stroud

Robert Franklin Stroud was born on 28 January 1890 and died 21 November 1963. He was known as the "Birdman of Alcatraz". He was one of the most notorious criminals in American history. While he was at Leavenworth Penitentiary he sold birds and became a respected ornithologist, but despite his nickname, he was not permittedto keep his birds during his stay at alcatraz, where he was incarcerated from 1942.

Born in Seattle, Washington, Stroud ran away from his abusive father at age 13, then at age 18, he became a pimp in Alaska. In January 1909, he shot and killed a barman who had attacked one of his prostitutes, Kitty O'Brien, after killing this barman, he turned himself in to the authorities. He was found guilty of manslaughter on 23 August 1909, and was sentenced to 12 years in the federal penitentary on Puget Sound's McNeil Island. Stroud had gained a reputation as a extremely dangerous inmate who frequently had confrontations with fellow inmates and staff, and on 26 March 1916, he stabbed one of the guards, Andrew F. Turner, as he took Stroud's visitation privilege to meet his younger brother. He was then convicted of first-degree murder and sentenced to execution by hanging, after several trials, Stroud's sentence was changed to life imprisonment.

In 1920, Stroud had found a nest of three injured sparrows in the prison yard, he began raising them, within a few years, he had acquired a collection of some 300 canaries. He began extensive research into them after being granted equipment by a radical prison-reforming warden. He made several contributions to the avian pathology, most notably a cure for the hemorrhagic septicemia family of diseases, gaining much respect and some level of sympathy among ornithologists and farmers.

Stroud's birds infuriated the prison staff, then he was transferred to Alcatraz in 1942, this was done after the staff discovered that he was secretly making alcohol using some of the equipment in his cell. Stroud then began his 17-year term at Alcatraz Federal Penitentiary on 19 December 1942, and he became inmate #594. He spent six years in segregation and the remaining 11 years in the prison hospital wing due to his health. His health began to decline, so therefore, he was transferred to the Medical Center for Federal Prisoners in Springfield, Missouri, where he stayed until his deat on 21 November 1963 at the age of 73.

From all of Stroud's activities, he created problems for the prison management. According to regulations of the prison, each letter sent or received at the prison had to be read, copied, and approved. Stroud was involved in his business that this alone required a full-time secretary. Additionally, most of the time, his birds were permitted to fly freely within his cells, because of the great number of birds he kept, therefore, this made his cell filthy all the time.

Stroud had intensified the efforts of the prison at Leavenworth to transfer him out of Leavenworth. Stroud, however, had discovered a Kansas state law that forbade the transfer of prisoners that were married in Kansas. To this end, he married Della Mae Jones by proxy, this infuriated the prison's administrators, who would not allow him to correspond with his wife. Stroud's mother, Elizabeth Stroud, believed that women were nothing but trouble for her son.

On 19 December 1942, Stroud was finally transferred to Alcatraz Federal Penitentiary being inmate #594. Before leaving Leavenworth to head to Alcatraz, he was given 10 minutes with his birds. With the strict regulations that Alcatraz has, Stroud's birds and equipment was sent to his brother.

Stroud is considered to be one of the most notorious criminals in American history. Robert Niemi states that Stroud had a "superior intellect," and became a "first-rate ornithologist and author," but was an "extremely psychopath, disliked and distrusted by his jailers and fellow inmates." however, by his last years, he was seen more favorably, and Judge Becker considered Stroud to be modest, no longer a danger to society, with a genuine love for birds. Given his level of notoriety, the crimes he committed were unremarkable, especially as the assaults he committed has a clear cause.

In 1963, Richard M. English, a young lawyer who campaigned for Kennedy in California, took to the cause of securing Stroud's release. He met with former President Harry Truman to enlist support, bt Truman declined. He also met with senior Kennedy-administration officials who were studying the subject. English took the last photo of Stroud, in which he is shown with a green visor. The warden of the prison attempted to have English prosecuted for bringing something into the prison he did not take out: unexposed film. The authorities declined to take any action. Upon Stroud's death, his personal property, including original manuscripts, was delivered to English, as his latest legal representative, who later turned over some of the possessions to the Audubon Society.

CHAPTER THREE

James "Whitey" Bulger

James Joseph "Whitey" Bulger, Jr. was born on 3 September 1929. He is a former organized crim figure from South Boston, Massachusetts, United States. Based on grand jury testimony from Kevin Weeks' former associates, U.S. prosecutors indicted Bulger for 19 murders.

In 1943, Bulger was a 14-year-old boy and was arrested for larceny. He later was arrested for assault, battery and armed robbery. He was then sentenced to a juvenile reformatory. After his release in 1948, he joined the United States Air Force. In 1950 he was arrested for going awall (absent withut leave). After that time, he got a dishonorable discharge in 1952 and returned back to Massachusetts.

In 1956, Bulger was sentenced to federal time at Atlanta Penitentiary for armed roberry and hijacking. For eighteen months, Bulger and eighteen other inmates, all of whom had volunteered to lessen their sentences, were given LSD and other drugs. Bulger later complained that he and other inmates had been "recruited by deception" and that they were told that they were helping to find "a cure for schizophrenia".

He was later transferred from Atlanta Penitentiary to Alcatraz Federal Penitentiary, arriving on 2 November 1959, as prisoner #AZ1428. He became a close friend of fellow inmate Clarence Carnes, alias "The Choctaw Kid". In November 1962, he was transferred to Leavenworth and in the following year, 1963, to Lewisburg Federal Penitentiary. He was released in 1965, after serving nine years in prison.

After the 1972 truce, Bulger and the Mullens were in control of South Boston's criminal underworld. FBI Special Agent Condon noted in his log in September 1973, that Bulger and Nee had been heavily shaking down the neighborhood's bookmakers and loansharks. During the years that followed, Bulger began to remove opposition by persuading Howie Winter to sanction the killings of those who "stepped out of line". In a 2004 interview, Winter recalled that the highly intelligent Bulger, "could teach the devil trucks." During this era, Bulger's victims included Mullen Gang veterans Spike O'Toole, Paulie McGonagle and Tommy King.

In 1971, the FBI, searching for reliable information in their battle against the Patriarca crime family, approached Bulger and attempted to recruit him as an informant. FBI Special Agent Dennis Condon was assigned to make the pitch. However, Condon reported that Bulger was too concerned about his own safety to start working with the FBI.

In 1974, Bulger became partners with Stephen Flemmi, an Italian American mobster and FBI informant since 1965. Although it is a documented fact that Bulger soon followed Flemmi's example, exactly how and why continues to be debated. Special Agent John Connolly frequently boasted to his fellow agents about how he recruited Bulger at a late night meeting at wollaston Beach inside an FBI issue car. Connolly allegedly said that the Bureau could help in Bulger's feud with Mafia underboss Gennaro Angiulo. After listening to the pitch, Bulger is said to have responded, "Alright, if they want to play checkers, we'll play chess. Fuck 'em."

In 1997, after Bulger and Flemmi had been informants that had been disclosed, Weeks met with retired FBI Agent John Connolly, whom had shown him a FBI informant file on Bulger. In order to explain Bulger and Flemmi's status as informants, Connolly said "The Mafia was going against Jimmy and Stevie, so Jimmy and Stevie went against them."

A federal judge ruled on 5 September 2006, that the mishandling of Bulger and Flemmi caused the 1984 murder of informant John McIntyre. As a result, the McIntyre family was ordered to receive more than $3 million from the U.S. Federal Government. The judge stated the FBI failed to properly supervise their own agent John Connolly, who was convicted and sent to jail in 2002, had also failed to investigate numerous allegations that Bulger and Flemmi were involved in drug trafficking, murder, and other crimes for decades.

When consolidating power, in 1979, the FBI pursuaded federal prosecutors to drop all charges against Bulger and Flemmi. Bulger and Flemmi then took over the remnants of the Winter Hill Gang and used their status as informants to eliminate competition. The information they supplied to the FBI is subsequent years was responsible for the imprisonment of several of Bulger's associates whom Bulger viewed as threats; however, the main victim of their relationship with the federal government was the Italian-American Patriarca crime family, which was based in Boston's North End, and in Federal Hill, Providence. After the 1986 RICO indictment of underboss Gennaro Angiulo and his associates, the Patriarca family's Boston operations were in a shambles.

In 1980, Bulger was approached in South Boston's Triple O's saloon by Louis Litif, a neighborhood bookmaker. Kevin Weeks, who was then a bouncer at Triple O's, witnessed a discussion. According to Weeks, Litif had been stealing from his partners in the bookmaking operation and using the money to traffic cocaine. What is more, Litif has not only refused to pay a cut of his drug profits, but had also committed two murders without Bulger's permission. As Weeks listened, Litif told an outraged Bulger that he was also going to kill his partner, "Joe the Barber," whom falsely accused him of stealing money from the bookmaking operation. Bulger refused to sanction this, but Litif vowed to kill him anyway. Seething with anger, Bulger informed Litif, "You've stepped over the line. You're no longer just a bookmaker." Litif responded that, as Bulger was his friend, he had nothing to worry about. Bulger icily responded, "We're not friends anymore, Louie." At the time Kevin Weeks was about to get married to his high school sweetheart, Pamela Caveleri. A short time before the wedding, Weeks informed Bulger that he was having difficulty seating Louis Litif. "Don't worry about it," Bulger responded.

In 1982, a South Boston cocaine dealer named Edward Brian Halloran, known on the streets as "Balloonhead," approached the FBI and stated that he had witnessed Bulger and Flemmi murdering Louis Litif. Meanwhile, FBI agent John Connolly kept Bulger and Flemmi closely briefed on what Halloran was falsely claiming involvement in their assassination of Tulsa, Oklahoma businessman Roger Wheeler. Ultimately, the FBI discovered Halloran's falsehoods and refused him and his family a place in the Witness Protection Program. Soon after, on 11 May 1982, Bulger, Flemmi and Weeks were tipped off that Halloran had returned to South Boston. As Michael Donahue and Edward Halloran drove out of the parking lot, Weeks signaled Bulger by stating, "The balloon is in the air," over a hand-held radio. Bulger drove up with a masked man armed with a silenced Mac 10; Bulger himself carried a .30 caliber carbine. Bulger, wearing a floppy hat and a long-haired wig, and the other shooter opened fire and sprayed Halloran and Donahue's car with bullets. Donahue was shot in the head and killed instantly. Halloran lived long enough to identify his attacker as James Flynn, a Winter Hill associate, who was later tried and acquitted. Flynn remained the prime suspect until 1999, when Weeks agreed to cooperate with investigators and identified Bulger as one of the shooters. Stephen Flemmi has identified the second shooter as Mullen Gang leader Patrick Nee. Nee denies the allegation and no chargers had yet to be filed. Michael Donahue was survived by his wife and his three sons. The Donahue and Halloran families eventually filed a civil lawsuit against the United States Federal Government after learning that FBI Agent John Connolly had informed Bulger of Halloran's informant status. Both families were awarded several million dollars in damages. However, the verdict was overturned on appeal, due to the late filing of the claims. Thomas Donahue, who was eight years old when his father was murdered, has become a spokesman for the families of those allegly murdered by the Winter Hill Gang.

In 1994, a joint task force of the Drug Enforcement Agency (DEA), the Massachusetts State Police, and the Boston Police Department launched a probe of Bulger's gambling operations. The FBI, by this time considered compromised, was not imformed. After a number of bookmakers agreed to testify to having paid protection money to Bulger, a Federal case was built against him under the RICO Act.

The last confirmed sighting of Bulger before his capture was in London 2002. However, there were unconfirmed sightings elsewhere. FBI agents were sent to Uruguay to investigate a lead. FBI agents were also sent to stake out the 60th memorial of the Battle of Normandy celebrations, as Bulger is reportedly an enthusiastic fan of military history. Later reports of a sighting in Italy in April 2007 proved false. Two persons on video footage shot in Taormina, Sicily, formerly thought to be Bulger and his lover, Catherine Greig, walking in the streets of the city center, were finally identified as a tourist couple from Germany. In 2010, the FBI turned its focus to Victoria, Britsh Columbia, on Vancouver Island. In pursuit of Bulger, a known book lover, the FBI visited bookstores in the area, questioned employees, and distributed wanted posters. Following his arrest, Bulger revealed that he had in fact traveled frequently. Also following his arrest, it was clear that he had not been reclusive, witnesses coming forward to say they had seen him on the

Santa Monica Pier and elsewhere in southern California. A confirmed report by an off-duty Boston police officer after a San Diego screening of *The Departed* also led to a search in Southern California.

After 16 years of being at large and 12 years on the FBI Ten Most Wanted Fugitives list, Bulger was arrested in Santa Monica, California, on 22 June 2011. Bulger was captured as a result of the work of the Bulger Fugitive Task Force, which consisted of FBI Agents and a Deputy US Marshall. According to retired FBI agent Scott Bakken, "Here you have somebody who is far more sophisticated than some 18-year-old who killed someone in a drive-by. To be a successful fugitive you have to cut all contacts from your previous life. He had the means and kept a low profile.

Authorities received a tip from a woman in Iceland that Bulger was living in a Santa Monica, California, apartment near a beach. Bulger was charged with murder, "conspiracy to commit murder, extortion, narcotics distribution and money-laundering." Agents found "more than $800,000 in cash, 30 firearms and fake IDs" at the apartment. Carmen Ortiz, U.S. attorney for the District of Massachusetts, said "she believes the death penalty is not an option in the federal charges Bulger faces in her district, but that he could face the death penalty for all his crimes.

Chapter Four

George "Machine Gun" Kelly

George Celino Barnes was born on 18 July 1895 and dies 18 July 1954. He was known as "Machine Gun Kelly". He was an American gangster from the prohibition era. He's mostly famous crime ws the kidnapping of a oil tycoon and businessman, Charles Urschel in 1933. He set the randsom for the release of Urschel at $200,000. Their victim had collected and left considerable evidence that assisted the subsequent FBI investigation that eventually led to Kelly's arrest in Memphis, Tennessee, on September 26, 1933.[3] His crimes also included bootlegging and armed robbery.

During the Prohibition era of the 1920s and 1930s Kelly worked as a bootlegger for himself as well as a colleague. After a short time, and several run-ins with the local Memphis police, he decided to leave town and head west with his girlfriend. To protect his family and escape law enforcement officers, he changed his name to George R. Kelly. He continued to commit smaller crimes and bootlegging. He was arrested in Tulsa, Oklahoma, for smuggling liquor onto an Indian Reservation in 1928 and sentenced for three years to Leavenworth Penitentiary, Kansas, beginning February 11, 1928. He was reportedly a model inmate and was released early. Shortly thereafter, Kelly married Kathryn Thorne, who purchased Kelly's first machine gun and went to great lengths to familiarize his name in the underground crime circles; she also helped plot some small bank robberies.

Nonetheless, Kelly's last criminal activity proved disastrous when he kidnapped a wealthy Oklahoma City resident, Charles F. Urschel and his friend Walter R. Jarrett. Urschel, having been blindfolded, made note of evidence of his experience including remembering background sounds, counting footsteps and leaving fingerprints on surfaces in reach. This proved invaluable for the FBI in their investigation, as they concluded that Urschel had been held in Paradise, Texas, based on sounds that Urschel remembered hearing while he was being held hostage.

An investigation conducted at Memphis disclosed that the Kellys were living at the residence of J. C. Tichenor. Special agents from Birmingham, Alabama, were immediately dispatched to Memphis, where, in the early morning hours of September 26, 1933, a raid was conducted. George and Kathryn Kelly were taken into custody by FBI agents and Memphis police. Caught without a weapon, George Kelly allegedly cried, "Don't shoot, G-Men! Don't shoot, G-Men!" as he surrendered to FBI agents. The term, which had applied to all federal investigators, became synonymous with FBI agents. The couple was immediately removed to Oklahoma City. The arrest of the Kellys was overshadowed by the escape of ten inmates, including all of the members of the future Dillinger gang, from the penitentiary in Michigan City, Indiana, that same night.

On October 12, 1933, George and Kathryn Kelly were convicted and sentenced to life imprisonment. The trial was held at the Post Office, Courthouse and Federal Office Building in Oklahoma City. Investigation in Coleman, Texas, disclosed that the Kellys had been housed and protected by Cassey Earl Coleman and Will Casey and that Coleman had assisted George Kelly in storing $73,250 of the Urschel ransom money on his ranch. This money was located by Bureau agents in the early morning hours of September 27 in a cotton patch on Coleman's ranch. They were both indicted at Dallas, Texas, on October 4, 1933, charged with harboring a fugitive and conspiracy, and on October 17, 1933, Coleman, after entering a plea of guilty, was sentenced to serve one year and one day, and Casey after trial and conviction, was sentenced to serve two years in the United States Penitentiary at Leavenworth, Kansas.

The kidnapping of Urschel and the two trials that resulted were historic in several ways. They were: 1) the first federal criminal trials in the United States in which movie cameras were allowed to film; 2) the first kidnapping trials after the passage of the so-called Lindbergh Law, which made kidnapping a federal crime; 3) the first major case solved by J. Edgar Hoover's FBI; and 4) the first prosecution in which defendants were transported by airplane.

Machine Gun Kelly spent his remaining 21 years in prison. During his time at Alcatraz he got the nickname "Pop Gun Kelly". This was in reference, according to a former prisoner, to the fact that Kelly was a model prisoner and was nowhere near the tough, brutal gangster his wife made him out to be. He spent 17 years on Alcatraz as inmate number 117, working in the prison industries, and boasting of and exaggerating his past escapades to other inmates, and was quietly transferred back to Leavenworth in 1951. He died of a heart attack at Leavenworth on July 18, 1954, his 59th birthday, and is buried at Cottondale Texas Cemetery with a small headstone marked "George B. Kelley 1954".

Chapter Five

Rafael Cancel Miranda

Rafael Cancel Miranda was born July 18, 1930 is a political activist, member of the Puerto Rican Nationalist Party and an advocate of Puerto Rican independence. On March 1, 1954, Cancel Miranda together with fellow Nationalists Lolita Lebron, Andres Figueroa Cordero, and Irving Flores Rodriguez entered the United States Capitol building armed with automatic pistols and fired 30 shots. Five congressmen were hit, however all the representatives survived and Cancel Miranda, along with the other three members of his group were immediately arrested. Cancel Miranda was the only nationalist out of the four to have been jailed in Alcatraz Federal Penitentiary, a Federal Bureau of Prisons federal prison.

Cancel Miranda was born in the City of Mayagüez, located in the western coast of Puerto Rico. His father, Rafael Cancel Rodríguez, was president of the Mayagüez chapter of the Puerto Rican Nationalist Party and his mother was a member of the Daughters of Freedom, a non-partisan women's organization which was the women's branch of the Nationalist Party. His father, a businessman and owner of a furniture store, had been imprisoned because of his political beliefs.

In March 1937, when Cancel Miranda was seven years old, he and his family traveled to the City of Ponce to participate in a march organized by the Puerto Rican Nationalist Party. The march, which was scheduled for March 30 (Palm Sunday), was organized to commemorate the ending of slavery in Puerto Rico by the governing Spanish National Assembly in 1873, and to protest the incarceration by the U.S. Government of Nationalist leader Pedro Albizu Campos on sedition charges.

Upon learning of the planned protest, however, the colonial Governor of Puerto Rico at the time, General Blanton Winship, who had been appointed by US President Franklin Delano Roosevelt, demanded the immediate withdrawal of the permits. They were withdrawn a short time before the march was scheduled to begin. As "La Borinqueña", Puerto Rico's national song, was being played, the demonstrators began to march. They were then fired upon for over 15 minutes by the police from their four positions. About 235 people were wounded and nineteen were killed.[3] Among the dead were 17 unarmed civilians and two police officers at the hands of the Insular Police for a total of 19 dead, in addition 235 civilians were wounded, including women and children. Ultimately, responsibility for the massacre fell on Governor Winship, and he is considered to have, in effect, ordered the massacre.[4] Many were chased by the police and shot or clubbed at the entrance of their houses as they tried to escape. Others were taken from their hiding places and killed. Leopold Tormes, a member of the Puerto Rico legislature, told reporters how a policeman murdered a nationalist with his bare hands. Dr. Jose N. Gandara, one of the physicians who assisted the wounded, testified that wounded people running away were shot, and that many were again wounded by the clubs and bare fists of the police. No arms were found in the hands of the civilians wounded, nor on the dead ones. About 150 of the demonstrators were arrested immediately afterward; they were later released on bail. The incident is known as the Ponce Massacre.

The white nurse's uniform of Cancel Miranda's mother was soaked with blood as she crawled over bodies in search of her husband. Miraculously, they both managed to return home unharmed. After the family returned home, Cancel Miranda committed his first political act in his first grade class in school when he refused to salute the American flag which at the time was mandatory.

Cancel Miranda joined the "Cadets of the Republic", the youth organization of the Nationalist Party, and organized nationalist youth committees in different towns. His group had a radio program and a small newspaper. As a cadet, Cancel Miranda went to welcome Albizu Campos in December 1947, when the Nationalist Party leader returned from the United States after serving out a ten-year prison sentence - first in the U.S. penitentiary in Atlanta, then in New York - on charges of conspiracy to overthrow the U.S. government and "inciting rebellion" against it. Following World War II, there was widespread resistance to Washington's attempt to impose English as the main language of instruction in Puerto Rico's schools. Cancel Miranda was among those who participated in a school strike to this respect, two months before his graduation, Miranda was expelled from school. He then went to San Juan to finish high school.

Puerto Ricans became U.S. citizens as a result of the 1917 Jones-Shafroth Act and those who were eligible, with the exception of women, were expected to serve in the military, either voluntarily or as a result of the military draft. In 1948, Cancel Miranda, then eighteen and in high school, refused to be drafted into the military. One day, he was walking to school in San Juan with other students, and there was a car with four FBI agents at the corner of his house. He handed his books to the other students to take them to the place where he was living. The men arrested him and charged him with refusing the U.S. draft. The U.S. Federal Court in Puerto Rico sentenced him to two years and one day and he was sent to a prison in Tallahassee, Florida, where he remained from 1949 to 1951. During his stay in prison he confronted a prison guard because of the racist segregation inside prison walls. Under Jim Crow legislation at the time, the prison dormitories were segregated.

In the 1950s, the United States entered the Korean War. Believing that he was to be drafted by the US Military and that he would once again face a prison term for refusing, Cancel Miranda followed the advice of his wife and his sister Zoraida and went into a self exile in Cuba. Cancel Miranda arrived in the city of Santiago using a different identity, Rafael Rodríguez. Cuba at that time was governed by Carlos Prio Socarras. He moved to Havana where, with the help of Albizu Campos' son, Pedro Albizu Campos Meneses, he found a job with the Public Works Department. After a while, he went to work for the Raymond Concrete Pipe Co. which was building the Línea Street Tunnel, which connects the two banks of the Almendares River.

On October 30, 1950, a Nationalist Party uprising occurred in Puerto Rico. The uprising was a call for independence against United States Government rule of Puerto Rico. It was also a protest against the approval of the creation of the political status the "Free Associated State of Puerto Rico" or how it is legally known, the "Commonwealth of Puerto Rico" ("Estado Libre Associado") for Puerto Rico which was considered a colonial farce. Numerous Nationalists were arrested, among Cancel Miranda's father. In 1951, he published an article in a Havana paper to commemorate the first anniversary of that uprising. The United States embassy learned about it and demanded that the Prío Socarrás government turn him over along with another Puerto Rican, Reynaldo Trilla, but the Cuban authorities ignored them.

Aracelio Azcuy, a politician of the Civil Damages Office and supporter of Prio Socarras, used to asked Cancel Miranda to campaign for him, to write his speeches. On March 10, 1952, Fulgencio Batista led a military coup overthrowing Prío Socarrás' government. After the coup, Batista's police arrested Cancel Miranda and Trilla. They were sent to the Tiscornia prison until August 1952, when they both were expelled from Cuba.

In July 1954, Cancel Miranda, inmate number 1163, was sent to Alcatraz where he served six years of his sentence. Alcatraz island became a Federal Bureau of Prisons federal prison in August 1934 and was used as such for 29 years. There he worked in the brush factory and served as an altar boy at Catholic services. His closest friends were fellow Puerto Ricans Emerito Vasquez and Hiram Crespo-Crespo. They spoke Spanish and watched out for each other. On the recreation yard he often played chess with Harlem gangster Ellsworth "Bumpy" Johnson.[18] He also befriended Morton Sobell, they developed a friendship that lasts to this day.

His family made trips to San Francisco to visit him, however he wasn't allow to see his children. His wife was allowed to talk to him through a glass in the visiting room, using a phone. They were not allowed to speak in Spanish and had to speak in English. Cancel Miranda was a model prisoner and in 1960, after six years on Alcatraz, he was transferred to Leavenworth.

Cancel Miranda authored seven books and remains active in the struggle for Puerto Rican independence. He continues to carry the cause of freedom to other countries, and returns occasionally to the United States on speaking tours on behalf of Puerto Rican political prisoners. In 2006, he was awarded the José Martí Order by the Cuban government for his work. It is the highest honor Cuba accords to non-Cubans.[18] In 1979. at the International Conference in Support of Independence for Puerto Rico, held in Mexico City, Cancel Miranda. Irvin Flores Rodríguez, Lolita Lebrón and Oscar Collazo before representatives of some fifty-one countries they were seen as the embodiment of the directive of their teacher Albizu Campos to exercise valor and sacrifice.

A musical production of his poetry, "Por Las Calles de Mi Patria," has been enthusiastically received in Puerto Rico and in the United States. The poems are those he had sent to his father while in prison. He had thought them lost, and was surprised to find them published by his father. The musical production is dedicated to those active in the struggle for freedom.

Oscar López Rivera founded the Rafael Cancel Miranda High School in Chicago, in his honor. The school is now known as the Dr. Pedro Albizu Campos High School and the Juan Antonio Corretjer Puerto Rican Cultural Center.

Chapter Six

Bumpy Johnson

Ellsworth Raymond Johnson (October 31, 1905 – July 7, 1968) — known as "Bumpy" Johnson — was an American mob boss and bookmaker in New York City's Harlem neighborhood. The main Harlem associate of the Genovese crime family, Johnson's criminal career has inspired films and television.

Johnson was from Charleston, South Carolina on October 31, 1905. Johnson derived his nickname "bumpy" from a bump on the back of his head.[1] When he was 10, his older brother, Willie, was accused of killing a white man. Afraid of a possible lynch mob, his parents mortgaged their tiny home to raise money to send Willie up north to live with relatives.[2] As Johnson became older, his parents worried about his short temper and insolence toward whites and in 1919 he was sent to live with his older sister Mabel in Harlem.

Johnson was an associate of numbers queen Madame Stephanie St. Clair.

By the age of 30, Johnson had spent nearly half his life in prison for a variety of crimes. After being released from prison in 1932, Johnson learned that notorious gangster Dutch Schultz, who was known as the Beer Baron of the Bronx, had moved in on the numbers racket in Harlem. Any numbers banker who refused to turn over his numbers operation to Schultz was targeted for violence. Schultz was murdered in 1935, which was arranged by Lucky Luciano and the national crime syndicate.

Luciano took over most of Schultz's number operations in Harlem, but made a deal with Johnson which allowed the bankers who had fought for their independence to remain independent as long as their taxes were paid. That deal made Johnson an instant hero in the eyes of many Harlemites. Who were impressed that a black man could actually cut deals with the Italian Mafia.

Johnson was soon the toast of Harlem, and became friends with many Harlem luminaries such as Bill "Bojangles" Robinson, Ethel Waters, Cab Calloway, Lena Horne, Billie Holiday, and Sugar Ray Robinson. He also became sort of an unofficial crime boss of Harlem; no one could conduct criminal activities in his section of New York without first going through him.

In 1948 he met 34-year-old Mayme Hatcher at Frasier's Restaurant on Seventh Avenue in Harlem; the two were married six months later.

By the summer of 1952, Johnson's activities were being reported in the celebrity people section of *Jet*,[4] an American weekly marketed toward African American readers, founded in 1951 by John H. Johnson of Johnson Publishing Company in Chicago, Illinois.[5] That same year, Johnson was indicted in New York for conspiracy to sell heroin (he claimed to have been framed, and many people believed him) and was sentenced to fifteen years in prison. Two years later, *Jet* reported in its crime section that Johnson began his sentence after losing an appeal. He served the majority of his prison time at Alcatraz Prison in San Francisco Bay, California as inmate No. 1117, and it has been said that he helped three fellow inmates escape by arranging to have a boat pick them up once they broke out and made it to the San Francisco Bay. Johnson was released from prison in 1963 and returned to Harlem, where he was greeted with an impromptu parade.

Johnson was arrested more than 40 times and would eventually serve three prison terms for narcotics-related charges. In December 1965, Johnson staged a sit-down strike in a police station, refusing to leave, as a protest against their continued surveillance. He was charged with "refusal to leave a police station" but was acquitted by a judge.

Johnson was under a federal indictment for drug conspiracy when he died of heart failure on July 7, 1968 at age 62. He was at Wells Restaurant in Harlem shortly before 2 a.m., and the waitress had just served him coffee, a chicken leg, and hominy grits, when he keeled over clutching his chest. Childhood friend Finley Hoskins was there, and someone ran down the street to the Rhythm Club to get another childhood friend, Junie Byrd. When Byrd arrived, he cradled Bumpy in his arms, and Johnson briefly opened his eyes and smiled, then fell into unconsciousness. He was taken, by ambulance, to Harlem Hospital where he was pronounced dead. He is buried in Woodlawn Cemetery.

Chapter Seven

Mickey Cohen

Meyer Harris "Mickey" Cohen (September 4, 1913 – July 29, 1976) was a gangster based in Los Angeles and part of the Jewish Mafia, and also had strong ties to the American Mafia from the 1930s through 1960s.

Mickey Cohen was born on September 4, 1913, into an Orthodox Jewish family living in the Jewish Brownsville section of Brooklyn. His mother Fanny, who'd become widowed in September 1914, had emigrated from Kiev, Ukraine. At the age of six, Mickey was selling newspapers on the street; his brothers Louie or Harry would drop him off at his regular corner, Soho and Brooklyn Streets. Soon, however, Fanny moved her family to Los Angeles. In 1922, petty crime landed Mickey in reform school there.

As a teenager, Cohen began boxing in illegal prizefights in Los Angeles. In 1929, the fifteen-year-old moved from Los Angeles to Cleveland to train as a professional boxer. His first professional boxing match was on April 8 1930 against Patsy Farr in Cleveland, Ohio. It was one of the preliminary fights on the card for the Paul Pirrone/Jimmy Goodrich feature bout. On April 11, 1933 Cohen fought against Chalky Wright in Los Angeles, California. Wright won the match and Mickey was incorrectly identified as "Mickey Cohen from Denver, Colorado" in the *Los Angeles Times* sports page report. His last fight was on May 14, 1933 against Baby Arizmendi in Tijuana, Baja California, Mexico. On June 12, 1931 Cohen fought and lost a match against World Featherweight Champion Tommy Paul, having been knocked out cold after 2:20 into the first round. It was during this round he earned the moniker *"Gangster Mickey Cohen".* In Cleveland, Cohen met Lou Rothkopf, an associate of Moe Dalitz. Cohen later moved to New York, where he became associates with Tommy Dioguardi, the brother of labor racketeer Johnny Dio, and with Owney Madden. Finally, Cohen went to Chicago, where he ran a gambling operation for the Chicago Outfit, Al Capone's powerful criminal organization.

During Prohibition, Cohen moved to Chicago and became involved in organized crime working as an enforcer for the Chicago Outfit, where he briefly met Al Capone. During this period Cohen was arrested for his role in the deaths of several gangsters in a card game that went wrong.

After a brief time in prison, Cohen was released and began running card games and other illegal gambling operations. He later became an associate of Mattie Capone, Al's younger brother. While working for Jake Guzik, Cohen was forced to flee Chicago after an argument with a rival gambler.

In Cleveland, Cohen again worked for Lou Rothkopf, an associate of Meyer Lansky and Benjamin "Bugsy" Siegel. However, there was little work available for Cohen in Cleveland, so Rothkopf arranged for him to work with Siegel in California.

In 1939, Mickey Cohen was sent to Los Angeles by Meyer Lansky and Lou Rothkopf to work under Bugsy Siegel. During their association, Mickey helped set up the Flamingo Hotel in Las Vegas and ran its sports book operation. He also was instrumental in setting up the race wire, which was essential to Vegas betting. In 1947, the crime families ordered the murder of Siegel due to his mismanagement of the Flamingo Hotel, most likely because Siegel or his girlfriend Virginia Hill were skimming money. According to one account which does not appear in newspapers, Cohen reacted violently to Siegel's murder. Entering the Hotel Roosevelt, where he believed the killers were staying, Cohen fired rounds from his two .45 caliber semi-automatic handguns into the lobby ceiling and demanded that the assassins meet him outside in ten minutes. However, no one appeared and Cohen was forced to flee when the police arrived.

Cohen's violent methods came to the attention of state and federal authorities investigating the Dragna operations. During this time, Cohen faced many attempts on his life, including the bombing of his home on posh Moreno Avenue in Brentwood. Cohen soon converted his house into a fortress, installing floodlights, alarm systems, and a well-equipped arsenal kept, as he often joked, next to his 200 tailor-made suits. Cohen briefly hired bodyguard Johnny Stompanato before Stompanato was killed by actress Lana Turner's daughter. Cohen bought a cheap coffin for Stompanato's funeral and then sold Lana Turner's love letters to Stompanato to the press.

In 1950, Mickey Cohen was investigated along with numerous other underworld figures by a US Senate committee known as the Kefauver Commission. As a result of this investigation, Cohen was convicted of tax evasion in June 1951 and sentenced to prison for four years.When he was released in October 1955, he started again, and became an international celebrity. He sold more newspapers than anyone else in the country, according to author Brad Lewis· His appearance on television with Mike Wallace in May 1957 rocked the media establishment. He ran floral shops, paint stores, nightclubs, casinos, gas stations, a men's haberdashery, and even drove an ice cream van on San Vicente Boulevard in the Brentwood section of Los Angeles, according to author Richard Lamparski.

In 1957 *Time* magazine wrote a brief[2] about Mickey Cohen meeting with Billy Graham. Cohen said, "I am very high on the Christian way of life. Billy came up, and before we had food he said—What do you call it. that thing they say before food? Grace? Yeah, grace. Then we talked a lot about Christianity and stuff." Allegedly when Mickey did not change his lifestyle, he was confronted by some Christian acquaintances. His response: "Christian football players, Christian cowboys, Christian politicians; why not a Christian gangster?"

In 1961, Cohen was again convicted of tax evasion and sent to Alcatraz. He was the only prisoner ever bailed out of Alcatraz; his bond was signed by U.S. Supreme Court Chief Justice Earl Warren. After his appeals failed, he was sent to a federal prison in Atlanta, GA. His heavily armored Cadillac from this period was confiscated by Los Angeles Police Department and is now on display at the Southward Car Museum in New Zealand.[3] During his time on "the Rock," another inmate attempted to kill Cohen with a lead pipe. In 1972, Cohen was released from the Atlanta Federal Penitentiary, where he had spoken out against prison abuse. He had been misdiagnosed with an ulcer, which turned out to be stomach cancer. After undergoing surgery, he continued touring the U.S., including television appearances, once with Ramsey Clark.

Cohen's girlfriend Liz Renay herself spent three years in prison for refusing to inform on him. One of his many other girlfriends, Candy Barr, served prison time for marijuana possession. Two of his other favorites were Tempest Storm and Beverly Hills, the former having her breasts insured with Lloyd's of London. Mickey Cohen died in his sleep in 1976 and is interred in the Hillside Memorial Park Cemetery in Culver City, California. Cohen's extended family number many cousins who today reside in Wisconsin, New Jersey, New York, Florida, Washington, Vermont and California.

Chapter Eight

Arthur "Doc" Barker

Arthur R. Barker, born June 4, 1899 and died January 13, 1939. was an American criminal, the son of Ma Barker and a member of the Barker-Karpis gang along with Alvin Karpis.

Arthur Barker, better known as alias Doc Barker or Claude Dade was born in Aurora, Missouri to George Elias Barker and Ma Barker née Clark. Through the 1920s and 1930s, Barker, with his brother Fred and Alvin Karpis, committed numerous crimes such as theft, robbery, murder, and kidnapping.

On July 18, 1918 Doc Barker was arrested for stealing a car on the highway and was sent to serve prison time in Joplin, Missouri. On February 19, 1920 Arthur Barker escaped prison in Joplin, Missouri.

On August 25, 1921, night watchman Thomas Sherill was murdered by burglars at a hospital construction site in Tulsa, Okla. On January 14, 1922 Doc Barker was convicted of this murder and sentenced to a life term at McAlester prison in Oklahoma. He was paroled ten years later, on September 10,1932.

On December 16, 1932 Doc Barker participated in the robbery of the Third Northwestern Bank in Minneapolis. Two policemen were killed in that robbery and a civilian was murdered during the getaway. Doc Barker also helped the gang kidnap two wealthy St. Paul, Minnesota men: William Hamm in June 1933 and Edward Bremer in January, 1934. The FBI arrested Doc Barker on the streets of Chicago on January 8, 1935 and he was subsequently convicted of the Bremer kidnapping.[5] On January 16, 1935, Fred and Ma Barker were killed by the police and a year later Arthur Barker with Alvin Karpis were sent to Alcatraz. Barker became Alcatraz inmate 268-AZ in 1936. Barker with Henri Young and Rufus McCain attempted escape from Alcatraz on the night of January 13, 1939. The attempt failed. Barker was shot and killed by the guards; Young and McCain were recaptured and sent to solitary confinement.

Arthur Barker is buried in Olivet Memorial Park, Colma, California.

Chapter Nine

Alvin "Creepy" Karpis

Alvin Francis Karpis, born Albin Francis Karpowicz; August 10, 1907and died August 26, 1979, a Depression-era gangster nicknamed "Creepy" for his sinister smile and called "Ray" by his gang members, was a Canadian born (naturalized American) criminal of Lithuanian descent known for being one of the three leaders of the Barker-Karpis gang in the 1930s. He was the last "Public Enemy #1" to be taken. He also spent the longest time as a federal prisoner in Alcatraz Prison, serving twenty-six years.

Karpis was born to Lithuanian immigrants named John and Anna Karpowicz in Montreal, Quebec and was raised in Topeka, Kansas. He started in crime at about age 10, selling pornography and running around with gamblers, bootleggers, and pimps. In 1926, he was sentenced to 10 years at the State Industrial Reformatory in Hutchinson, Kansas for an attempted burglary. He escaped with another inmate Lawrence De Vol and went on a year-long crime spree, interrupted briefly while he lived with his parents after De Vol was arrested. After moving to Kansas City, Missouri, he was caught stealing a car and sent back to the Reformatory. Transferred to the Kansas State Penitentiary in Lansing, he met Fred Barker, who was in prison for bank burglary. Barker was one of the notorious members of the "Bloody Barkers", as the newspapers of the time had called them. The Barker family included the brothers Herman, Lloyd, Arthur or "Doc", and Fred, the sons of Ma Barker. Growing up impoverished in a sharecropping family, all the boys soon turned into hardened criminals, robbing banks and killing without provocation. Doc was sentenced to life imprisonment in 1920 after murdering a night watchman. Herman committed suicide on August 29, 1927, after being badly injured in a shootout with police in Wichita, Kansas following the robbery of the Newton Ice Plant in Newton, Kansas with Charles Stalcup and Porter Meeks. Lloyd was sentenced to 25 years in 1922, for mail theft and released in 1938; he was a US Army Cook at a POW camp and then was murdered by his wife in 1949. Ma did her part to help her sons. "Ma" Barker was not herself a criminal, but did nevertheless badger parole boards, wardens, and governors for the release of her boys when they were incarcerated. After Alvin was released in 1931, he joined up with Fred Barker in Tulsa, Oklahoma, and they soon put together the Karpis-Barker gang.

The Karpis-Barker gang became one of the most formidable criminal gangs of the 1930s. They did not hesitate to kill anyone who got in their way, even innocent bystanders. On December 19, 1931, Karpis and Fred Barker killed Sheriff C. Roy Kelley, who was investigating their robbery of a store in West Plains, Missouri. The gang, including Ma Barker and her paramour Arthur Dunlop, fled to St. Paul, Minnesota.

In 1933, on the same weekend as the Kansas City Massacre, they kidnapped William Hamm, a millionaire Minnesota brewer. His ransom netted them $100,000. Shortly after this, they abducted Minnesota banker Edward Bremer, whose ransom brought them $200,000. The group was led by Alvin, who had a photographic memory and was described as "super-smart" by fellow gang member Fred Hunter. The other leaders were Doc and Fred, both now out of prison, and the gang included about 25 others. At this time a myth was started that Ma Barker ruled the gang with an iron fist, but the facts do not seem to support these claims. It is highly unlikely that criminals as adept as Karpis, and even Ma's sons for that matter, would have listened to her. Karpis later wrote about this subject in his memoirs:

> "Ma was always somebody in our lives. Love didn't enter into it really. She was somebody we looked after and took with us when we moved city to city, hideout to hideout. It is no insult to Ma's memory that she just didn't have the know-how to direct us on a robbery. It would not have occurred to her to get involved in our business, and we always made it a point of only discussing our scores when Ma wasn't around. We'd leave her at home when we were arranging a job, or we'd send her to a movie. Ma saw a lot of movies."

Harvey Bailey, another well-known bank robber of the era knew the Barker gang well, and in his autobiography published in the 1970s, he agreed with Karpis, observing that Ma Barker "couldn't plan breakfast", and was certainly no mastermind behind any gang activity. It is purported that Ma Barker's entire reputation as a criminal mastermind was concocted by Hoover to protect the FBI's public image after federal agents discovered they had killed a 62 year old mother.

The kidnappings, however, would lead to the gang's end. The father of the kidnapped Edward Bremer was a friend of president Franklin D. Roosevelt. FDR had even mentioned the kidnapping in one of his fireside chats and, fueled also by the Lindbergh kidnapping, the FBI and local police bureaus greatly stepped up their pursuit of those engaged in these types of crimes. The FBI had by this time organized a group of highly skilled agents called the "flying squads", who specialized in hunting down the leading public enemies, and much progress was being made. The year 1934 alone saw the deaths of John Dillinger, Bonnie and Clyde, Charles "Pretty Boy" Floyd, Lester "Baby Face Nelson" Gillis, John "Red" Hamilton, Homer Van Meter, Tommy Carroll, and Eddie Green.

Just after Ma and Fred's death on January 16, 1935, Karpis nearly met his own violent end when the FBI located him in Atlantic City, New Jersey. Karpis and Harry Campbell managed to shoot their way to an escape, though Karpis' eight-month-pregnant girlfriend Dolores Delaney was hit in the thigh by a wild shot fired by Campbell. He continued his crimes with others, but had to be on the move more than ever as he was the fourth and last Public Enemy left (the previous three having been killed). He did manage to pull off a crime that echoed times of the "Old West", a train robbery in Garrettsville, Ohio, which netted $27,000. After the death of Ma and Fred, Karpis sent word to J. Edgar Hoover that he intended to kill Hoover the way Hoover had killed Ma and Fred. According to Karpis in *The Alvin Karpis Story*, the threat of death against Hoover turned out to be a rumor started by J. Edgar Hoover.

The FBI had come a long way since its reorganization and renaming in 1935 (from the Bureau of Investigation, created in 1908). J. Edgar Hoover was appointed as the acting head of the Bureau in 1924 and completely transformed the agency. Despite its successes, however, the agency had many problems. In those days, when the application of science and technology to fight crime was still in its infancy, the agency was at the mercy of public citizens for information. Often agents were sent off to remote locales that turned out to be red herrings due to bad information. The personal low point for Hoover came at an April 1936 United States Senate hearing. Senator Kenneth McKellar of Tennessee lambasted Hoover for the performance of the FBI and the fact that Hoover himself had never personally arrested anyone. After the hearing, a determined Hoover vowed he would capture Karpis personally.

Hoover would not have to wait long. On May 1, 1936, the FBI located Karpis in New Orleans, and Hoover flew there to be in charge of the arrest. As a dozen or so agents swarmed over Karpis' car, Hoover announced to Karpis that he was under arrest. A couple of versions of the arrest are reported. Karpis' version of the story, told in his memoirs, was that Hoover came out only after all the other agents had him seized. Only then did the agents call to Hoover that it was safe to approach the car. The official FBI version states that Hoover reached into the car and grabbed Karpis before he could reach a rifle in the back seat (in fact, the car, a Plymouth coupe, had no back seat). The scene was further confused when Hoover told his men to "put the [hand]cuffs on him." Not one agent had brought handcuffs. Karpis was tied up with the necktie worn by one of the agents. The capture of Karpis catapulted Hoover into the public eye, and made his name synonymous with law enforcement until he died in 1972 at the age of 77.

The capture of Karpis essentially ended the age of the big-name Depression Era criminals. In addition to those mentioned earlier, others killed violently in the 1930s were Jack "Legs" Diamond, Vincent "Maddog" Coll, Frank "Jelly" Nash and Dutch Schultz. Al Capone was in Alcatraz and slowly going insane from syphilis. The country had gradually started to recover from the Depression, law enforcement agencies had improved as well.

Karpis was brought to trial at the St. Paul Federal Courts Building (now called Landmark Center). Karpis initially pleaded not guilty. But as the case was called for trial, "Thomas J. Newman, attorney for Karpis, told the court his client, one of the actual kidnappers of Hamm, desired to plead guilty." Two weeks later Karpis offered "through his attorney, Thomas Newman, to plead guilty to the Bremer conspiracy" if kidnapping charges were dropped; the court accepted the offer.

Sentenced to life imprisonment, Karpis was incarcerated at the recently formed Alcatraz federal penitentiary from August 1936 to April 1962. For six months in 1958, he had been transferred to the Leavenworth federal penitentiary, but was then returned to Alcatraz. His main job at Alcatraz was working at the bakery. He was far from a model prisoner, frequently fighting with other inmates. Karpis served the longest sentence of any prisoner at Alcatraz (26 years). In April 1962, with Alcatraz in the process of being closed, he was transferred to McNeil Island Penitentiary in Washington state. While at McNeil, Karpis met a young Charles Manson. Karpis wrote about Manson in his autobiography with Robert Livesey (1980):

“This kid approaches me to request music lessons. He wants to learn guitar and become a music star. “Little Charlie” is so lazy and shiftless, I doubt if he'll put in the time required to learn. The youngster has been in institutions all of his life — first orphanages, then reformatories, and finally federal prison. His mother, a prostitute, was never around to look after him. I decide it's time someone did something for him, and to my surprise, he learns quickly. He has a pleasant voice and a pleasing personality, although he's unusually meek and mild for a convict. He never has a harsh word to say and is never involved in even an argument."

After Manson had become somewhat proficient on the guitar, he asked Karpis for help in getting a job playing in Las Vegas as Karpis had contacts with nightclub and casino owners there. Manson told him he would be bigger than the Beatles, but Karpis decided to leave Manson on his own regarding his music career.

Karpis was released on parole in 1969 and deported to Canada, although he initially had difficulty obtaining Canadian passport credentials, having had his fingerprints removed by underworld physician Joseph Moran in 1934. He settled in Montreal.

He wrote his first memoirs in 1971 and published another memoir book in 1980. During his first book tour across Canada for *Public Enemy Number One* for McClelland & Stewart (published in the United States as *The Alvin Karpis Story*), Karpis, looking more like an accountant than a gangster, still showed a wry sense of humor. In Edmonton, Alberta, while shuffling Karpis between various interviews with the media, M&S book rep Ruth Bertelsen made a stop at her bank. Asking Karpis if he wanted to come in with her, Karpis replied "No dear, you take care of the vault, I'll drive." He became a mentor to her young son until the sociopathy of some of his advice to her child angered Miss Bertelsen.

He moved to Spain in 1973. On August 26, 1979 he died by what was originally ruled suicide by authorities, as sleeping pills were found by his body, but later it was ruled death from natural causes. Some closer to the scene say foul play may have been involved. Robert Livesey, who co-wrote Karpis's 1979 book, said Karpis was not the type to have committed suicide. Livesey said Karpis was a survivor, having served 33 years in prison, and also stated Karpis was anticipating the publication of the book. Livesey believed Karpis had been introduced to pills and alcohol by his last girlfriend Nancy, to give a relaxing high and perhaps Karpis accidentally over-indulged on one occasion, with fatal consequences. No autopsy was performed and Karpis was buried the next day in Spain.

Chapter Ten

Al Capone

Alphonse Gabriel "Al" Capone (/æl kəˈpoʊn/; born January 17, 1899 and died January 25, 1947) was an American gangster who led a Prohibition-era crime syndicate. The Chicago Outfit, which subsequently also became known as the "Capones", was dedicated to smuggling and bootlegging liquor, and other illegal activities, such as prostitution, in Chicago from the early 1920s to 1931.

Born in the borough of Brooklyn in New York City to Italian immigrants, Capone became involved with gang activity at a young age after having been expelled from school at age 14. In his early twenties, he moved to Chicago to take advantage of a new opportunity to make money smuggling illegal alcoholic beverages into the city during Prohibition. He also engaged in various other criminal activities, including bribery of government figures and prostitution.

Despite his illegitimate occupation, Capone became a highly visible public figure. He made donations to various charitable endeavors using the money he made from his activities, and was viewed by many to be a "modern-day Robin Hood". Capone's public reputation was damaged in the wake of his supposed involvement in the 1929 Saint Valentine's Day Massacre, when seven rival gang members were executed.

Capone was convicted on federal charges of tax evasion in 1931 and sentenced to federal prison; he was released on parole in 1939. His incarceration included a term at the then-new Alcatraz federal prison. In the final years of Capone's life, he suffered mental and physical deterioration due to late-stage neurosyphilis, which he had contracted in his youth. On January 25, 1947, he died from cardiac arrest after suffering a stroke.

Alphonse Gabriel Capone was born in the borough of Brooklyn in New York on January 17, 1899. His parents, Gabriele Capone (December 12, 1864 – November 14, 1920) and Teresina Raiola (December 28, 1867 – November 29, 1952), were immigrants from Italy. His father was a barber from Castellammare di Stabia, a town about 16 mi (26 km) south of Naples, and his mother was a seamstress and the daughter of Angelo Raiola from Angri, a town in the Province of Salerno.

Gabriele and Teresa had nine children: Alphonse "Scarface Al" Capone, James Capone (who later changed his name to Richard Hart and became, ironically, a Prohibition agent in Homer, Nebraska), Raffaele Capone (also known as Ralph "Bottles" Capone, who took charge of his brother's beverage industry), Salvatore "Frank" Capone, John Capone, Albert Capone, Matthew Capone, Rose Capone, and Mafalda Capone (who married John J. Maritote). His two brothers, Ralph Capone and Frank Capone worked with him in his empire. Frank did so until his death on April 1, 1924 and Ralph ran the bottling companies (both legal and illegal) early on, and was also the front man for the Chicago Outfit for some time until he was imprisoned for tax evasion in 1932. The Capone family immigrated to the United States, first immigrating from Italy to Fiume, Austria–Hungary (now Rijeka, Croatia) in 1893, traveling on a ship to the U.S. and finally settled at 95 Navy Street, in the Navy Yard section of downtown Brooklyn. Gabriele Capone worked at a nearby barber shop at 29 Park Avenue.[5] When Al was 11, the Capone family moved to 38 Garfield Place in Park Slope, Brooklyn.

Capone showed promise as a student, but had trouble with the rules at his strict parochial Catholic school. He dropped out of school at the age of 14, after being expelled for hitting a female teacher in the face. He worked at odd jobs around Brooklyn, including a candy store and a bowling alley. During this time, Capone was influenced by gangster Johnny Torrio, whom he came to regard as a mentor.

After his initial stint with small-time gangs that included the Junior Forty Thieves and the Bowery Boys, Capone joined the Brooklyn Rippers and then the powerful Five Points Gang based in Lower Manhattan. During this time, he was employed and mentored by fellow racketeer Frankie Yale, a bartender in a Concy Island dance hall and saloon called the Harvard Inn. After he inadvertently insulted a woman while working the door at a Brooklyn night club, Capone was attacked by her brother, Frank Gallucio, and his face was slashed three times on the left side. These scars gave him the nickname "Scarface", a nickname he despised.[4] Yale insisted that Capone apologize to Gallucio, and later Capone hired him as a bodyguard.[9][10] When photographed, Capone hid the scarred left side of his face saying the injuries were war wounds. Capone was called "Snorky", a term for a sharp dresser, by his closest friends.

On December 30, 1918, at age 19, Capone married Mae Josephine Coughlin, who was Irish Catholic and who, earlier that month, had given birth to their first son, Albert Francis ("Sonny") Capone. As Capone was under the age of 21, his parents had to consent to the marriage in writing.

Capone departed New York for Chicago without his new wife and son, who joined him later. In 1923, he purchased a small house at 7244 South Prairie Avenue in the Park Manor neighborhood on the city's south side for US$5,500.

Capone was recruited for Chicago by Johnny Torrio, his Five Points Gang mentor. Torrio had gone there to resolve some family problems his cousin's husband was having with the Black Hand and killed them. He saw many business opportunities in Chicago, especially bootlegging following the onset of prohibition. Chicago's location on Lake Michigan gave access to a vast inland territory, and it was well-served by railroads. Torrio took over the crime empire of James "Big Jim" Colosimo after he was murdered. Yale was a suspect, but legal proceedings against him were dropped due to a lack of evidence. Capone was suspected in the murders of Colosimo and two other men. He was seeking a safe haven and a better job to provide for his new family.

The 1924 town council elections in Cicero became known as one of the most crooked elections in the Chicago area's long history of rigged elections, with voters threatened by thugs at polling stations. Capone's mayoral candidate won by a huge margin and weeks later announced that he would run Capone out of town. Capone then met with his puppet-mayor and knocked him down the town hall steps.

For Capone, the election victory was also marred by the death of his older brother Frank at the hands of the police. Capone cried at his brother's funeral and ordered the closure of all the speakeasies in Cicero for a day as a mark of respect.

Much of Capone's family settled in Cicero as well. In 1930, Capone's sister Mafalda married John J. Maritote at St. Mary of Częstochowa, a massive Neo-Gothic edifice towering over Cicero Avenue in the Polish Cathedral style.

The Torrio-Capone organization, as well as the Sicilian-American Genna crime family, competed with the North Side Gang of Dean O'Banion. In May 1924, O'Banion discovered that their Sieben Brewery was going to be raided by federal agents and sold his share to Torrio. After the raid, both O'Banion and Torrio were arrested. Torrio's people murdered O'Banion in revenge on October 10, 1924, provoking a gang war.

In 1925, Torrio was severely injured in an attack by the North Side Gang; he turned over his business to Capone and returned to Italy. During the Prohibition Era, Capone controlled large portions of the Chicago underworld, which provided The Outfit with an estimated US$100 million per year in revenue. This wealth was generated through numerous illegal vice enterprises, such as gambling and prostitution; the highest revenue was generated by the sale of liquor.

His transportation network moved smuggled liquor from the rum-runners of the East Coast, The Purple Gang in Detroit, who brought liquor in from Canada, with help from Belle River native Blaise Diesbourg, also known as "King Canada", and local production which came from Midwestern moonshine operations and illegal breweries. With the revenues gained by his bootlegging operation, Capone increased his grip on the political and law-enforcement establishments in Chicago. He made his headquarters at Chicago's Lexington Hotel; after the St. Valentine's Day Massacre, it was nicknamed "Capone's Castle".

The organized corruption included the bribing of Chicago Mayor William "Big Bill" Hale Thompson, and Capone's gang operated largely free from legal intrusion. He operated casinos and speakeasies throughout the city. With his wealth, he indulged in custom suits, cigars, gourmet food and drink (his preferred liquor was Templeton Rye from Iowa[21]), jewelry, and female companionship. He garnered media attention, to which his favorite responses were "I am just a businessman, giving the people what they want", and "All I do is satisfy a public demand". Capone had become a celebrity.

His rivals retaliated for the violence of Capone's enforcement of control. North Side gangsters Hymie Weiss and Bugs Moran wanted to bring him down. More than once, Capone's car was riddled with bullets. On September 20, 1926, the North Side gang shot into Capone's entourage as he was eating lunch in the Hawthorne Hotel restaurant. A motorcade of ten vehicles, using Thompson submachine guns and shotguns riddled the outside of the Hotel and the restaurant on the first floor of the building. Capone's bodyguard, Frankie Rio, threw him to the ground at the first sound of gunfire. Several bystanders were hurt from flying glass and bullet fragments in the raid. Capone paid for the medical care of a young boy and his mother who would have lost her eyesight otherwise. This event prompted Capone to call for a truce, but negotiations fell through. The attacks were believed to have been made at Moran's direction and left Capone shaken.

Capone placed armed bodyguards around the clock at his headquarters at the Lexington Hotel, at 22nd Street (later renamed Cermak Road) and Michigan Avenue. For his trips away from Chicago, Capone was reputed to have had several other retreats and hideouts in places including Couderay, Wisconsin.

Capone's Couderay hideout (a popular tourist attraction in later years) is a 407-acre property, complete with a 37-acre lake which reputedly was used to land planes filled with illegal liquor for shipment south to Chicago. Former New York gang member Owney "The Killer" Madden retired to Hot Springs and invited his former colleagues to visit him there; this was also the place that Lucky Luciano was first arrested. As a further precaution, Capone and his entourage would often show up suddenly at one of Chicago's train depots and buy up an entire Pullman sleeper car on night trains to places such as Cleveland, Omaha, Kansas City, Little Rock or Hot Springs, where they would spend a week in luxury hotel suites under assumed names. In 1928, Capone bought a 14-room retreat on Palm Island, Florida, close to Miami Beach.

The St. Valentine's Day Massacre eliminated some of Capone's enemies, but outraged the general public

It is believed that Capone ordered the 1929 Saint Valentine's Day Massacre in the Lincoln Park neighborhood on Chicago's North Side. Details of the killing of the seven victims in a garage at 2122 North Clark Street (then the SMC Cartage Co.) and the extent of Capone's involvement are widely disputed. No one was ever brought to trial for the crime. The massacre was thought to be the Outfit's effort to strike back at Bugs Moran's North Side gang. They had been increasingly bold in hijacking the Outfit's booze trucks, assassinating two presidents of the Outfit-controlled *Unione Siciliana*, and made three assassination attempts on Jack McGurn, one of Capone's top enforcers.

To monitor their targets' habits and movements, Capone's men rented an apartment across from the trucking warehouse that served as a Moran headquarters. On the morning of Thursday February 14, 1929, Capone's lookouts signaled gunmen disguised as police to start a "raid". The *faux* police lined the seven victims along a wall without a struggle then signaled for accomplices with machine guns. The seven victims were machine-gunned and shot-gunned. Photos of the massacre victims shocked the public and damaged Capone's reputation. Federal law enforcement worked to investigate his activities.

Al Capone's cell at the Eastern State Penitentiary, Philadelphia, PA

In 1929, the Bureau of Prohibition agent Eliot Ness began an investigation of Capone and his business, attempting to get a conviction for Prohibition violations. Frank J. Wilson investigated Capone's income tax violations, which the government decided was more likely material for a conviction. In 1931 Capone was indicted for income tax evasion and various violations of the Volstead Act (Prohibition) at the Chicago Federal Building in the courtroom of Judge James Herbert Wilkerson.[24] His attorneys made a plea deal, but the presiding judge warned he might not follow the sentencing recommendation from the prosecution. Capone withdrew his plea of guilty.

His attempt to bribe and intimidate the potential jurors was discovered by Ness's men, The Untouchables. The *venire* (jury pool) was switched with one from another case, and Capone was stymied. Following a long trial, on October 17 the jury returned a mixed verdict, finding Capone guilty of five counts of tax evasion and failing to file tax returns (the Volstead Act violations were dropped). The judge sentenced him to 11 years imprisonment, at the time the longest tax evasion sentence ever given, along with heavy fines, and liens were filed against his various properties. His appeals of both the conviction and the sentence were denied. One of the Capone properties seized by the federal government was an armored limousine. The limousine was later used to protect President Franklin D. Roosevelt after the attack on Pearl Harbor.

In May 1932, Capone was sent to Atlanta U.S. Penitentiary, but he was able to obtain special privileges. Later, for a short period of time, he was transferred to the

Lincoln Heights Jail. He was transferred to Alcatraz on August 11, 1934, which was newly established as a prison on an island off San Francisco. The warden kept tight security and cut off Capone's contact with colleagues. His isolation and the repeal of Prohibition in December 1933, which reduced a major source of revenue, diminished his power.

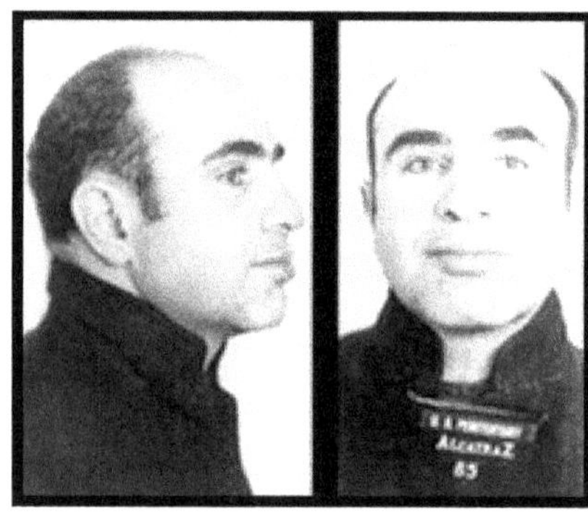

Al Capone at Alcatraz

During his early months at Alcatraz, Capone made an enemy by showing his disregard for the prison social order when he cut in line while prisoners were waiting for a haircut. James Lucas, a Texas bank robber serving 30 years, reportedly confronted the former syndicate leader and told him to get back at the end of the line. When Capone asked if he knew who he was, Lucas reportedly grabbed a pair of the barber's scissors and, holding them to Capone's neck, answered: "Yeah, I know who you are, greaseball. And if you don't get back to the end of that fucking line, I'm gonna know who you were."

Capone was admitted into the prison hospital with a minor wound and released a few days later.[3] In addition, his health declined as the syphilis which he had contracted as a youth progressed. He spent the last year of his sentence in the prison hospital, confused and disoriented. Capone completed his term in Alcatraz on January 6, 1939, and was transferred to the Federal Correctional Institution at Terminal Island in California, to serve the one-year contempt of court term he was originally sentenced to serve in Chicago's Cook County Jail. He was paroled on November 16, 1939, and, after having spent a short time in a hospital, returned to his home in Palm Island, Florida.

Capone's control and interests within organized crime diminished rapidly after his imprisonment. Additionally, 20 years of high living had seriously ravaged his health. He had lost weight, and his physical and mental health had deteriorated under the effects of neurosyphilis. In 1946, his physician and a Baltimore psychiatrist performed examinations and concluded that Capone, due to brain damage caused by the syphilis, then had the mental capability of a 12-year-old child.[35] He often raved about Communists, foreigners, and Bugs Moran, who he was convinced was plotting to kill him from his Ohio prison cell.

Unable to resume his criminal career, Capone spent the last years of his life at his mansion in Florida. On January 21, 1947, Capone had a stroke. He regained consciousness and started to improve but contracted pneumonia.

He suffered a fatal cardiac arrest the next day. On January 25, 1947 Al Capone died in his home, surrounded by his family, and was buried at Mount Carmel Cemetery in Hillside, Illinois.

CERTIFICATE OF DEATH

ALCATRAZ
Federal Prison of A Lifetime

www.ingramcontent.com/pod-product-compliance
Ingram Content Group UK Ltd.
Pitfield, Milton Keynes, MK11 3LW, UK
UKHW051133260726
13967UKWH00010B/3032

9 781304 806604